Jim Wortham

The Spring of Love

By Jim Wortham

Jim Wortham

James Wortham Publishing Company
P O Box 40
Madison, Indiana 47250-0040 U.S.A.

Email: JimWortham123@gmail.com

Autographed books may be ordered
direct from author.
See page 137 for order information.

The Spring of Love
Copyright © 2021 by Jim Wortham

Art via Unsplash, Pixabay, Pexels, Creative Market
Editor & Typesetter: Gypsy Mercer
Book & Cover Design: Gypsy Mercer

*Author's note: this is a work of fiction.   Names,
characters, places and incidents are a product of the
author's imagination. Any resemblance to actual people,
living or dead, or actual events is purely coincidental.*

The Spring of Love/Jim Wortham ~ First Edition
ISBN 978-1928877042

Library of Congress Control Number: 2021902344

Dedication

I have gone into my past and
dusted off the experiences
I have had and wrote them
out on pieces torn from
grocery sacks

I realize that you also have
your own unique collection
of highs and lows

Maybe our libraries of
experiences know each
other

Jim Wortham

Some Days Bring Sunshine

Jim Wortham

MAYBE

Maybe
just maybe
you were
the one
to complete
what I
was missing

Maybe
just maybe
you were
my soul mate

Maybe
just maybe
you
were the other
half of me

Maybe

COLORS

You brought so many
colors
to each
of my
days

Why
did you
take so long
to cross
       my

          path

      ?

ONE MOMENT

You

    and

        I

take one moment
at a time

    the way

        it should have

           always been

TOUCH AND GO

It is okay
to only see
each other
once in a while

It does not mean
I do not care
for you
or you do not care
for me
    It has been
        two years
            between touches

It means
we both have
    paths
        to walk
            down
It takes time
for our
paths
to come back around
and meet
again

Jim Wortham

FERRIS WHEEL

I saw you at a cotton candy stand
buying bubble gum flavored
cotton candy
I was standing nearby
you smiled
Asked if I would like
to taste your cotton candy
We road the roller coaster
the Ferris wheel
and as many rides
as we could pack into one day
Afterwards
we spent hours

sharing stories from our past
while enjoying the evening

I think
of that day and night
Did you enjoy it
as much as I did
?
Do you
think about it
as often as I do
?

MOODS

I want
to touch
you
before time
switches moods

I want
to say
    I love you
      I respect you
        You have made me
          a better person

HITCHHIKING

My old Chevy
purchased for $150
was broken down
It was old and slow
As date night arrived
I planned to hitchhike
to a dance and walked
to a busy highway
A police lady stopped and
asked if she could help
I smiled, said it was Friday
I wanted to go to a dance
and my car was in the shop
She wished me good luck
and winked good-bye

A fire-red Corvette slowed

a girl in her late teens

with a gorgeous smile

asked if I would like

to go for a ride

This was the beginning

of a dazzling relationship

I am not sure what changed

We stopped dating

maybe my Chevy

drove too slow

or her Corvette

drove too fast

The relationship ended

as quickly as it began

TRUTH

I finally told you
the truth
I said
I think I love you

You smiled
and said
Come and walk with me

LOVE IN WINTER

I stayed at a beach motel

looking for love

I walked the beach

I was lonely

She appeared out of nowhere

Said hello

She was looking for love

We spent many days together

at the beach

We dated a year

Distance apart

brought another man

into her life

And we drifted apart

My beautiful mermaid
if you read this
remember I loved you
that one winter

Jim Wortham

TICK TICK

It is winter
Even the sun
knows not to shine
into our window

We must have
  every space
    and
      each moment
to share
  with
    each
      other

But
  the clock
   has
    the
     nerve
      To tick...

SATURDAY NIGHT

Do you remember
        that night
            like I do
                ?
I went alone to watch four
Elvis Presley movies
for a dollar
You pulled your car
beside mine and waved
Knocked on my window
asking if I could use
some company
That night was beautiful
It was MAGICAL

That was the beginning

of many nights to come

Do you want to go again

?

There may be some place

we can watch movies

Come back into my life

and be my love

Jim Wortham

GOODBYE

I would like
to say
more
to you

Should I share
with you now
those little things
that seem
so important
when they come
to mind
?

I have learned
that being
too honest

saying too much
might make me
appear
ordinary
not mysterious enough
to keep another's interest

On the other hand
there is
the idea
that if
I shared more
and you saw
me clearer
you might
like me more

I have stopped
taking chances

I will
say goodbye
for now

but I promise
I will
be back

TOUCH ME AGAIN

Touch me now
Touch me a lot

We have been apart
for such a long time

So many others
brought us love
So many others brought us pain

Now our paths
combine again
We can start over
if we think we can

Love me again
Love me a lot
We can start over
if we think we can

Jim Wortham

WHITE PEBBLES

You walked before my eyes
when I least expected it
kicking white pebbles
down the sidewalk
while walking your dog

I did not know
how to go about
meeting you
I thought about
tripping you
but decided
to fill my lungs with air
and scream
Hi!

Jim Wortham

MY BED ON THE SEA

I gave it up
Possessions I spent
a third of my life
accumulating

Sure
it was difficult at first
the spirit of more, more, more
crept into me
like a disease

I had to operate to cut it out

I gave my possessions away
I was promised
by those who know

Freedom
would begin immediately

Now
having given all I have
to strangers
I make the sea my bed
and as the mystics promised
all my needs are met daily
I am freer
and more at peace
than I ever imagined
possible

Jim Wortham

OUR LIVES TOUCHED

I was afraid to ask your name

We met walking in a park

Our lives touched

for a few moments

then

the chance was gone

I still wonder

why

We did not give us

a chance

BOX OF KITTENS

Every day he was
strumming his guitar
singing his own songs

He kept a box nearby
with kittens in the box

Children laughed and played
with the kittens

I watched
people of all ages
stop and listen
captivated by
the singer's songs

They called him The Singer
He lived and slept in Central Park
He began strumming and singing
when the sun came up
hoping to be discovered

He sang

seven days a week

no matter the weather

He was hopeful

He was

living on a dream

His friends said his dream

would never come true

But The Singer never gave up

Seven years later

I returned

The Singer

was no longer singing in the park

I asked about him
I held back happy tears
as I was told
he was offered a record contract
and several albums later
all his dreams
finally came true
Singing the words he knew
in his heart

TOO SHY

I was afraid you would laugh
or walk away
if I asked to be your friend

Back then I
missed chances
to fall in love
or just have a friend
because I was afraid
to say the words
on the phone or
in person . . . those words,
can I be your friend?

It is easier now
Life has taught me
no one has to
have their feelings
hurt
If someone says no
next time bring a flower
and smile

Jim Wortham

FINDING THE RIGHT WORDS

You were laughing
with a handsome guy
No one I could compete with
I wondered why other guys
were so lucky
and I was
always unlucky

I noticed your
heavenly smile
and knew
I would never
have a chance
with you
Not ever

Then he left
You stood alone
I casually walked in
your direction
searching
for words to say

My throat became dry
The fear of being
turned down
returned

Not being good
with flattery
I simply said
You have a beautiful
smile

You looked into my eyes
and said
No one has ever
told me that before
I have heard a lot of
pick-up lines

You invited me
to have coffee
with you

You said
you're
kinda shy
Aren't you
?
I like that in a guy

Later
you asked if we
could go out on a date

Some Days Bring Rain

Jim Wortham

THE WORLD SPINS TOO FAST

The world spins too fast
for gentle people
My closest friends
ran the race
We were going to have it all
We grew tired
and did not keep
in step
Where was the race
to end up
?
Was there a basket of gold
or promise of health
or forever friends
?

It has been a while
a long while
since I started the race
I have slowed down

I sleep late now
don't get up before 10 am
or I sleep later
if the doorbell does not ring

Where are all the runners
in the race we started
?
The world spins
too fast

BROKEN PIECES

Can you
put me
back
together
and
discover
what
I was
like
before
I
broke
into
so
many
pieces
?

I WILL REMEMBER YOU

I did not
come by and visit
and bring you
the brownies and ice cream
you asked for

You waited
for weeks
for months
I planned to visit
as I had always done
being busy
got in the way

I don't know how long
it was before
you were gone

Too often
these days
I think of
getting together
and laughing
telling tales
like we used to do

The brownies
and ice cream
I planned to bring
never made it

I often wonder
if my neglect
caused you to
leave

THOUGHT OF YOU TODAY

The shovel
returns you
to dirt today

You will
sleep well

Better than
you ever did
on earth

THE TRIP

I heard about the trip
you have to take

.

.

.

and I am sorry

BEGIN AGAIN

Is there anything I can do

now

?

You left me with a letter

You said I did not seem to

love you enough

nor appreciate you

nor need you

How was I so blind

not to know you needed

reassurance that you are

my everything

?

Is it possible
we can begin again
?
I promise to
smother you with love
this time

Can we start over
please
?

DEEP BLUES

The news came today
Not on television
but from your best friend
You did not want to deliver
words saying you met
someone you love
more than
you ever loved me
I am locked out of your life

I know now why you stopped
answering my calls
I am sinking
into the blues
Deep, deep, deep blues
Not doing anything
My phone rings
unanswered

Not wanting to talk
Eating cheese and crackers
I am lonely
Lord, I am so lonely
Help me please
Help me
make it through the night

YOU LEFT WITHOUT A GOODBYE

It has happened

many times before

I was just a toss away

Someone to

love and leave

You gave me no warning

You did things to cause

me to love you

Knowing how to smile

Hold my hand

Share long kisses

Speak loving words

You left as quickly
as you entered my life

My world is spinning
This world is not gentle
with gentle people

Jim Wortham

THE SEASON OF LOVE

No
I do not want to leave you
but I must
you say
I see tears flowing from your eyes
Your parents said
we must say goodbye

Our nights were good
Better than good
They were jaw-dropping beautiful

While our love increased
without warning
your parents found a new man for you

Did you have a choice in this
?
You cut our relationship
with a single phone call
saying it was good
while it lasted
but it is over now

Did I mean so little to you
?
You meant the world to me

But thank you
Thank you for a season of love

Jim Wortham

WORDS THAT CAME TOO LATE

How can I reverse time

to tell you

all the things I meant

to say

?

How do I reverse time

after the final breath

to say I love you

I need you

I want you to be

part of my life

always

?

Jim Wortham

LAST NIGHT TOGETHER

I play back each word
within my mind
wondering what
caused our relationship
to crumble
before my eyes
Maybe it wasn't words
it may be that someone new
entered your life
and you felt I
wouldn't understand
and would only try
to talk you out of it

I sit alone tonight
blaming myself

In the days to come
if you discover what
caused
our relationship to break
that we could not
put back together
would you
write me a letter
so I'll know
?

Jim Wortham

SIESTA KEY

Years ago I went to
the Florida beaches
I became a beach bum

and
loved
it

I wrote poetry
   short stories
      started a novel

I thought this life
would last forever
with seagulls flying over
white sand to sleep on
friendly people

I could not afford to stay
or to come back later

I may not
    go
        back
           home

It did not last
I had bills to pay
making a living
the best way I could
I left paradise behind

OUR TURN

We missed our turn
to sit down
have a drink
get to know each other
start a relationship
We missed our turn
at love

Please understand
I did not feel good
about myself
since the last lady
said goodbye

Perhaps
I was so down on myself

I could not hear
any hint
that you were interested

My friend tells me that
you were once interested
that I
did not seem interested

We missed our turn
at something
that could have been

Jim Wortham

TWO NIGHTS

Our lives entwined
in a magical city
so many
yet so few
years ago

We wrote until
my letter
was returned
"Moved no forwarding address"
I had to give up on you

If you read this
remember our two special nights
together
?

I am wondering

can ESP

cause you to hear

my thoughts

tonight

?

Jim Wortham

LOOKING BACK

Maybe some relationships
are not worth renewing

Sometimes our day
is empty
Not much going on

We flip through pages
from our memory book and
think of calling
someone from our past

Is it worth it
to renew a relationship
with someone we are over
?

Is a need to fill a void
worth renewing
a wrong relationship
?

We are doing the best we can
at the moment
Each decision we make today
was made before
when facts were fresh

We did the best we could
Give yourself a break
We are not perfect
In that moment
we gave the best
we had to offer

Looking back

is easy

It always is

It is funny

when we realize

what

should have been done
after
too much time
has passed
to right a wrong

Looking back
    Looking back
        Looking back

There might have been
a better way

STAGES

Teen years
Sensitive
Inhibited
Threatened by every girl
I met
I felt I was not
good enough
for the girls I liked

Twenties
Wondered what was wrong
with me
because I could not keep
the women I dated

Early thirties
Working hard to pay bills
Angry at what the world had done
to make people rush so much
Better with women

Mid thirties
forcing myself to slow down
due to health reasons
Trying to stop
take time to enjoy life
I almost forgot
if it is even possible
Sensitivity is coming back
I am beginning again
to love people

Jim Wortham

YESTERDAYS

Do I remember
    Yes I remember
        my yesterdays
            quite well

Those were the days
when love came around
a little more often

Footsteps
of someone to love
come less often now
The footsteps are fainter
harder to hear

ALONE

I alone
    now remember
There was something
you urgently
wanted
to say to me
before I left

I alone
    now remember
A look in your eyes
A hope in your eyes
    that I would respond
to something you
wanted to say

I was hurried
trying to leave
Insensitive
to the expectancy
in your eyes

Tonight
I slow down
to remember
and hurt
giving way to tears
for your silenced
message

Jim Wortham

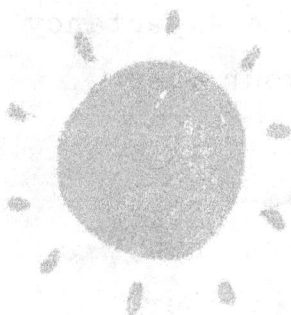

ECSTASY

Fleeting moments
of ecstasy
against boring
days and nights alone

Sometimes
a stranger
brings the ecstasy
when their touch touches mine

After they are gone
ecstasy remains on my mind
for awhile
maybe a day
maybe more

Then unwanted boredom
tires
my mind

Jim Wortham

FRIDAY NIGHT

Friday night
is
date night

It is now Friday night
At the mall
I see others
sitting
while waiting on a pay phone
to be free

I feel their hurt after
their call ends
They stand up
and walk slowly away

I guess whoever they called
had plans
other plans
that would not include them

It has always been this way
Lonely people
looking for someone
to pass the hours with
during the long weekends

SOLITARY DREAMER

Solitary dreamer
here
I return
to watch waves slap my feet

Years escaped
since I once built
dream castles
in the sky

Now
years
and years later
dreams
are harder to believe

LAST NIGHT

It is 11:30 pm
I look back
over the last
24 hours

Last night
same time
I sat here
writing
introspective thoughts

I was going to make
today a happier one
filled more with what
I wanted to do
but duties stole the time
happiness hid all day

Jim Wortham

Some Days Bring Reflection

Jim Wortham

LOVELY LADY

I remember when I was shy I would force myself to sit down where a lovely lady was sitting. I asked if I might join her....and if she could use a little company. Each time I was invited to enjoy a deep conversation. We often talked until midnight. That began the seeds of a loving relationship.

Over time I overcame shyness. I'm older now and I'm not so self-conscious. Even now, I've never been turned away when I ask a lovely lady...

Jim Wortham

CREATIVITY

Will it last
?
What
a question

Words flowed
without stopping

I wrote each word
not knowing what would follow
It was inspiration
as only inspiration can be
in its finest and purest
essence

Each day was filled with
emotions
that I would write about
Later
I strived to find a way to
turn these poems
into published books

Youth always finds a way
to make a way when there
appears to be no way

Maybe because
nothing is impossible
at that time of life

And the energy flows
the extra mile
until we reach
or
partly reach
our goals

Then the reality of life
knocks on our door

BROKEN DREAMS

I hope
to find the path
to my dreams.
I keep
grabbing the rope
to climb
to the dreams

Each time
I almost get there.
I let go
of the rope
too soon
or the rope becomes ragged
and breaks
I'm climbing again

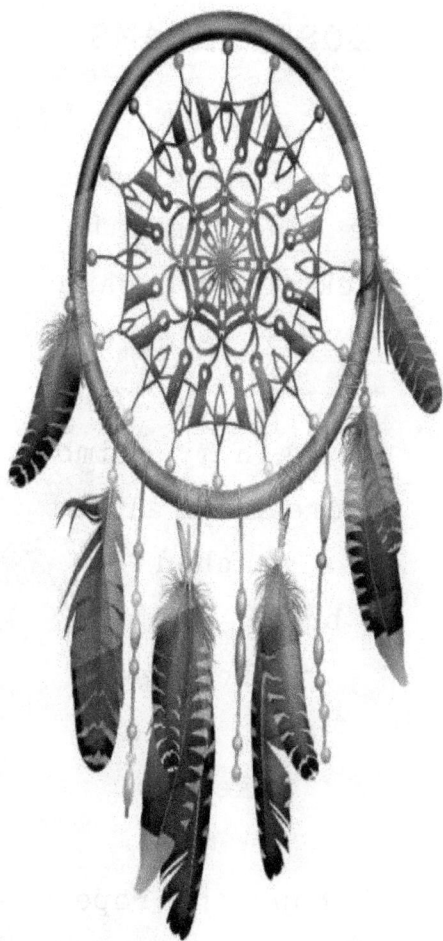

LOST DREAMS

I hope
to find the path
back to my dreams
I keep reaching
to grab the rope
to begin my climb
to dreams I almost
reached
but I let go
of the rope
that would
take me

I hope the rope
does not break
this
time

REGRETS

I cannot let my yesterdays

darken my life

my thoughts

I am not the same person

God, please forgive me

as I forgive others

In this body of clay

my spirit strives

to help and heal

I am broken

striving to be holy

Jim Wortham

I WILL NEVER KNOW

Was it something I said

or

Was it something I did

or

Is there someone new

After months of joy and laughter

you no longer answer my calls

Panic has sat in

I do not know what happened

Could it have been prevented

With tear drops falling on the floor

I turn on a recording

Ray Charles sings

It's crying time again

I listen to it
over and over again
Somehow I must find a way
to fall asleep

Jim Wortham

POEM MAKER KIT

I am at my favorite cafe
I ask the waitress for
napkins and a pencil
She brings a pile of napkins
with a sharpened pencil

For a dollar cup of coffee
and free refills
my creative thoughts
pour onto napkins
spilling words
to share with
you

POETRY ENGINE

After 3 poetry books published
last year, my poetry engine died.

My friend Ted tells me to get
my poetry engine started by
buying 4 or 5 kinds of tasty
liquor then sit down and drink
6 to 12 drinks until poetry
starts pouring out.

Sabrina says to have some
exciting experiences to see if
I can jump start my poetry engine.

She says she can suggest some experiences to get poems flowing once again.

Mikey says just sit for days with pencil and paper until the poetry bleeds from my veins.

Anybody anywhere have other ways to crank up my poetry engine? I need to keep my poetry engine running. I fear it will become rusty and cannot be fixed.

MAY I JOIN YOU TONIGHT

I want to share a little wisdom
that I've learned over the years.
I want to encourage you.

Don't give up on meeting people.
Especially don't give up on finding
love. You will find someone you can
enjoy and love.

Leave your safe place and circulate
and talk with everyone you feel led
to. They want a friend as much as
you do. And if you're lucky, and
the chemistry is right, your world
may be turned upside down, and your
happiness and their happiness will
become one.

NEIGHBORS

The man
who nobody talks with
was invited
to play
a game of horse-shoes

I saw him laugh
clap his hands
for the first time

SLOWING DOWN

After the rushing
all that rushing
    rushing to climb the career
ladder
    rushing to buy the best

Watching others
pass by
while I work

My mind
always wanting
    wanting this
    wanting that
Seeking security
        recognition

How many man-made gods
did I follow
    money
    recognition
    greed
        ?

Did I put these
in front
of the God I dedicated
my life to
    ?

I cannot bring
back those I loved
I cannot tell them
what I
want to say

I will slow down
    develop
        relationships
           with others
             and God

BE CAREFUL WITH ME

Be careful
not to rearrange me
into your idea
of a perfect person

I have traits you do not like
I know that

but what you consider bad
others may like

Allow me to remain
the person
that I am

IF I COULD REWIND TIME

That thought comes to
all of us sometimes
doesn't it
?
That we could redo
parts of our past
and have better outcomes
?
When I think about this
I wonder why I would choose differently
?

I made the choices
I thought were the best
I could not foresee the future
I made the best decisions
at the time

Tonight that thought
spins through my mind
if I could
rewind
time

Jim Wortham

ONCE IT WAS EASY

Years ago
it was easy
Life was fun
Writing poems was natural

I am now self-conscious
about each word I write
I wonder if the reader
will understand
what I am saying

Once I did not have these worries
I wrote how I felt
and it felt good
Now I am slow to share my thoughts
But it is coming back rapidly

I am feeling more confident
Spring is here

BACK A FEW YEARS AGO

I carried a travel bag
with clothes
going across the states
stopping at beach towns
staying
long enough to write
new poems
from a new beach
with new people I met

Too many years
ago
but I loved it

Life was easier then
people were easy
to make friends
and poems
were easy to
write

NO WORK, JUST PLAY

I took a basket of food
cheese
soft drinks
bread
crackers
mustard
and went to the beach
to chill out

I let all concerns
drift into
the sky

IT IS GOOD TO BE ALONE

Much should be said
about spending time
alone

I have been with others
so long
that I have forgotten
the peace
that comes
from being alone

To refresh my spirit
To collect my thoughts
To create a path for my future

DO NOTHING

Doing nothing
is
sometimes
what I need to do

Sometimes
doing nothing
is all I need to do

Sometimes
doing something
is wrong

Sometimes waiting
for an answer
in silence
is the right thing to do

A POET IS BORN

I could never

write a poem

until

you

entered

my life

At that
moment
a poet
was born

Jim Wortham

PLAYING LAZY

Today
doing nothing
but relaxing

Feeling good
about it

Been rushing
too much

I like this
day of calm

DEAD POETS

I am thinking of poets
I once knew
It is sad

Rod McKuen
Donald Hall
Peter McWilliams
Javan
Leonard Cohen
and others
who did not live forever

As a poet ages
he questions
the use
of writing more poems
getting another book
published

After all
no one will remember his
name after he is gone

Jim Wortham

When we are young
we think
we will never die

We all cross a line
as time passes
where we wonder
how soon we will die
and how should we spend
today and tomorrow

A reality check
Not
crying the blues

It is life

Just life

Some Days Bring Prayer

Jim Wortham

I CANNOT HEAR YOU

Hello Lord
can you hear my thoughts
?
The radio is loud
The TV is on all the time
Should I turn down the volume
?

I have been waiting to hear from you
To talk about
Things like what I should do and
if I should be friends
with people I recently met

I'm turning off the radio
and TV
and the noise in my mind
now

Sorry Lord that I was caught up
with all the noise of life
Please try talking with me again

Like you used to do

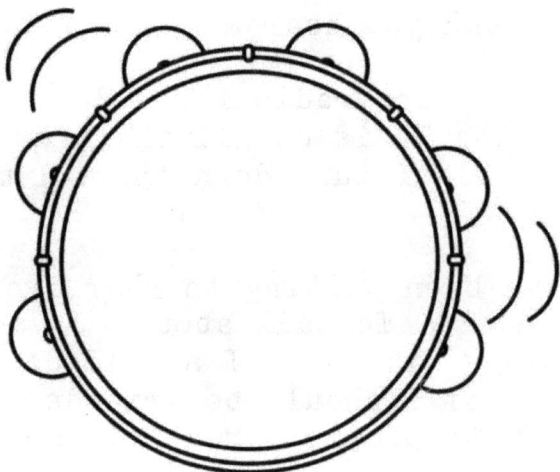

TAMBORINE GIRL

It was a cruel night
lightning flashed
thunder crashed
rain blinded my driving
I saw a light
from a small building
Stopped since the rain
filled the windshield
Then I heard music
Not sure why I did
I entered the building
being invited by the music

I had without knowing it
walked into a small church
I watched as a teenager
dressed in white
played a black wooden tambourine
with a white scarf hanging from it

Another girl
a few years older
was singing Amazing Grace

This is the part
I am unable to explain
The church was filled with
all ages of people
and as I watched

I was unable to move
I watched in slow motion
people going to the front
waiting for the preacher to pray
for those coming forward
Many stayed until I left

Without speaking to anyone
I walked to my car
feeling totally renewed

AN ANGEL SAT WITH ME

I never saw her before
I was eating with friends
They liked to laugh
and told clean jokes
When our food arrived
one asked
if he could say grace
We said of course
They left an hour later
I was sitting alone
when an angel
asked to join me
Yes, of course
She asked if I was a Christian
(how did she know?)
"Yes"
She continued

I have been watching you
and your friends

You all seem so different
She looked into my eyes
for what seemed minutes
and continued
You may be involved
with someone
but on the off chance you are not
may I leave you my name
and phone number
                    ?
This has happened only once
I was lonely then
The following years
were wonderful

SO MANY PEOPLE

Somehow
it feels good
to know
so many people
are
praying
and
that something
something
might just happen

WAITING

She sits on the beach at twilight
waiting for someone
anyone
with a friendly smile
and warm words
No one stops
She is not homeless
She has made her home
the beach
or nearby park where
she sleeps on sand
or a bench in the park
with newspapers
over her to stay warm

Once I stopped
and asked if she could
use a little company
She broke into tears
then said
no one ever offered
to sit with me
I learned her name

She asked to pray for me
taking my hand in hers
and praying a comforting prayer

As I think about her

tonight

I find myself

praying for her

remembering her holding my hand

Mentally I place her hand in mine

as I pray for her

and not for

myself

Jim Wortham

God

be

with us

The Seasons of Love Series

The Summer of Love $ 9.95

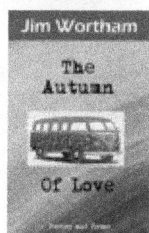

The Autumn of Love $ 9.95

The Winter of Love $ 9.95

The Spring of Love $ 9.95

Thank you for reading my book.
Autographed copies are available from
Jim Wortham, PO Box 40
Madison, Indiana 47250-0040 U.S.A.
Email: Jim Wortham123@gmail.com

Shipping within the United States is
$5 for the entire order. Contact me
for overseas shipping costs.

Jim Wortham

Follow Jim Wortham

Jim's blog: www.JimWorthamPoet.com
Facebook: www.facebook.com/Jim.Wortham.54
Jim's email: jimwortham123@gmail.com

Jim Wortham Poetry Books
Post Office Box 40
Madison, Indiana 47250-0040
U.S.A.

Autographed books available

www.ingramcontent.com/pod-product-compliance
Lightning Source LLC
Chambersburg PA
CBHW031515040426
42445CB00009B/238